THE THINGS I LEARNT AND THE THINGS I STILL DON'T KNOW ABOUT

TALITHA WING

WRECKING BALL PRESS

THE THINGS I LEARNT AND THE THINGS
I STILL DON'T KNOW ABOUT
Talitha Wing

ISBN 978-1-903110-83-6

First published in this edition 2021 by Wrecking Ball Press.

Copyright: Talitha Wing

Supported using public funding by
ARTS COUNCIL
ENGLAND
LOTTERY FUNDED

ACKNOWLEDGEMENTS:

this is dedicated to all the incredible women who have raised me, loved me, supported, challenged and changed me. And for my sister, Saphira who is the greatest woman I have ever known.

there aren't enough words in the world to thank you all, so here are just a few.

enjoy x

CONTENT

PART 1

BECOMING WOMAN

EASY PEELERS

orange is my
favourite colour

flavour

fruit

filled with reminders
of my youth

of peeling rinds
and orange juice

stained, sticky fingers
used

to pull apart segments

of citrus filled
sweetness

stinging in the cracks
of chapped lips

and pips
we had to be careful not to
choke on

i ate six once

despite my allergies
and had to go to a&e

with swollen eyes
itchy throat
a taste for danger

and fresh OJ.

C-SECTION

when i was little
i was really fascinated
by my own birth

for years i couldn't
imagine being cut out
like a picture plucked from my
mummy's tummy
like a ripe strawberry

the idea of a
C SECTION
was a complete mystery
to me

but

i've been thinking
you know
those days
that you're just not ready for

the pulled back curtain
bright light blizzard
barging it's way into your room
at the command of someone else's
hands

the window flung open
for the uninvited cold
to filter in and clasp
every inch of your
un-expectant torso

the way the day
forces itself in
dusts you off
holds you up
ready to present
to the world

now

i think it might have felt a
little like that.

TAMPONS

i passed him
the box of tampons
without meeting his eyes
as if i was a naughty school child

asked for a bag in a whisper
stuffed them into hiding

and left the shop
as if i was storing a bomb

i spent an hour
sat on the toilet
trying to figure out
how
to make one fit inside me

and waited
until no one was in the next cubicle
to wash the blood off my hands
like i'd committed a murder

the rest of the day was spent
trying to walk normally, so as to hide the
evidence.

KNITTING

i used to love to
watch her knit

she'd spend hours
looping and crossing
and carving
art
out of wool
she'd collected

her fingers were gentle
and firm at the same time
and she'd find
her way through
the most complicated
template

sometimes a whole day's
work would be undone
in an instant
and the morning after
she'd start again

i wanted to be that patient

but my clumsy heavy hands
got angry and i never managed
to piece it together
smoothly

it's all rather fragile
isn't it?

just
one pull with
a little
too much force
and it's already fraying

my two fingers
desperately
clinging to the threads
of life
i've spent years
weaving together
as they so easily
unravel in my palms

and the patterns
tangle, knot, tear
holes in the perfect
pathway planned out
until no one can tell
what it's meant to be anymore

she made it look so easy

knitting

and living

there was always a fix
a quick whiz of
the needle around and
back on itself, a way of stitching
it all back together
so it still looked beautiful

saying nothing was ever too broken
to be fixed

a scarf
a jumper
a heart

she had this way of making
the process almost
as pleasing as the final product
taking pride in every single
fuck up

i think living
is a bit like knitting

and i want to do it
the way she did.

BUTTERFLIES AND FIREWORKS

i don't think it's
true
what they say about
butterflies
in your stomach
because these were more like fireworks
and they weren't in my stomach
they were a little further down.

FRIZZY HAIR

the insults you made
about my frizzy hair

flew across the room
and got tangled in it

so i brushed
and brushed
and brushed
them all out

until it looked a little more like yours.

SECRET UNIVERSE

from
the first time
a boy
took a trip up
my skirt and explored
the secret universe
between my thighs
i knew it would never be a secret again.

GREATEST GIFT

in year 7
our teacher showed us
a video

that was a lot of blood, guts
and other unidentifiable liquids

gushing like the grand canyon

heavy breathing, wheezing
and screaming

lots of pushing and panting
and these metal sticks
(i can only describe as
those tong things
they serve spaghetti with)

then suddenly this
weird squashed
half human/half alien baby-thing

with a purple string
shooting from its belly button

and then

"it's a girl"
and more grand canyon like gushing

but this time
tears and snot and sweat

until the screen turned black
followed by this title that read

'CHILD BIRTH IS THE GREATEST GIFT'

i still remember thinking

how i'd rather get a nintendo
for my birthday.

BEING BOTH

when we studied the
civil rights movement
at school

i remember distinctly
the guilt and shame
sprawled across a lot of the white kids
faces

they recognised in themselves
the perpetrator

and i remember distinctly
the sadness and anger
draped across a lot of the black kids'
faces

they recognised in themselves
the victim

in the history books

the stories are always of the victim
or the perpetrator

but what if, like me
you descend from both?

DEAR SOCIETY

next to the sweet aisle
in Sainsburys

is a place i call

hell

a dark ally of shelves
laden with

DIET AIDS

bottles of poison

calling out to those
who pass by
with the promise
of "drink two a day"
and shrink your way
to a body more loveable

drugs dressed up
as lollipops
and smoothies decorated
with sale labels
that draw us in
like
hollywood's version
of the child catcher

magic teas
that take fat and spin it
into gold
as we are told to try these
'disappearing acts'
at home

for £4.99

every time i see
teens
with not yet fully
formed forms
roaming those aisles
freely
piling their baskets
sky high
as if it were
Woolworths pick and mix

i want to scream stop

stop

selling
slimming shakes
and 'fat-burning' pills
that make our insides ache
to young girls

who should instead be taught
not to put anything

that *burns*

inside their bodies.

SUPERHEROES

they're not all
like the ones you read about in
comic books

they don't fly
or climb the side of buildings
or save the planet whilst wearing lycra

they aren't SUPER human
at all

they don't have to be

because most of the time
being JUST human is enough.

COCA COLA ANXIETY

there's this thing
this fizzy
prickling feeling

in the pit of my stomach
that sometimes rumbles
the way bubbles do

in a bottle of coke

it rises, swirls
sticky and so sharp it makes me
feel sick, stuck

sort of like a giant hand
has plucked me off the shelf
shaken me up, squeezed on my insides
till the outside's misshapen

taken
every last bit of my breath
till i'm left
too much liquid
trapped in a bottle
too small

the lid like a lock
on the door of a room
i need to get out of

and when i do
i spill, spray over the edges
loudly, messily
and with far too much force

making everything a bit
sticky with my sadness
discoloured with my
discomfort and wet
with what at the time
i think is weakness

but i'm slowly learning
that the fizziest cokes
taste the sweetest.

GIRLS NIGHT

girls night
was littered with sex stories
sprinkled like sugar

on top of honesty hour

we sipped wine
and joked about spit or swallow

ate popcorn and
pondered penetration

watched movies
while musing over multiple orgasms
and laughed at how we all
faked it.

WHAT I WAS

i was not a human
all i was, was a vehicle
for your pleasure

a car you drove
to your own climax

and

the only thing
your 'dirty talk'
made me feel

was an urgent need to be clean.

MISTAKES

she got it all wrong

again

folded

into the cavity of
possible errors
that sat
waiting
to catch her out

head buried
in the sand
shame blocking
her airways
regret
like a riptide
she wanted to drown in

but the sea spat her out
again

she lay on the shore
breathless and tired

transforming

this time

into someone
stronger

you see
after a while

your mistakes will

reshape

they'll turn into wise eyes
that glisten with hindsight

and

lived in hands
ready to hold those

who are yet to make them.

WISH

if we
could do away

with all those wishes
we have made
for 'perfect body' cardboard cut outs
of the same
shape and size

then

in their place

we could find the space
and time
to marvel at the wonders

we already are.

SOLELY

it is
incredibly generous

to share
the pieces of your heart
with someone

as long as you remember

to keep
the most precious parts

solely

for you.

"REVENGE OUTFIT"

i learnt
about the
"revenge outfit"
on the scrunched up pages
of a magazine
in my dentist's waiting room

after my filling

i ran to the nearest shop
and bought something
three sizes too small
squeezed into it
like a sausage
in the skin

and called my friend on speed dial

told her to bring
the black eye liner with the glitter
and enough money
to buy entry
into
Tiger Tiger

i watched a YouTube tutorial
on 'bad girl make up'
whilst sipping Tesco's own vodka
from a bottle

and broke the seal
before i left the house

queued in the cold for an hour
refusing to wear a jacket
so as not to waste
the duck tape
pressing my boobs into the shape of a love heart

but you know what

even
in that red plunge neck dress,
smokey eye and dark purple lip

even
after the flick of the hair
the turn of the heel
and the strut away from the bar
where you stood
choking on my insults

whilst watching me walk away
(probably kicking yourself)

it still hurt the same

because this pain was never about you

it was always about me.

KINDNESS

i know
that when the world
bites down
on your self worth

it is incredibly hard
to remain kind

but try to let
your words be filled with it
anyway

it is the best anti venom
to that kind of poison.

DRNK LVE

when you're
5 drinks in
and she

whispers

i love you

make sure
you take her
with a pinch of salt

the same way
you take your

tequila.

LET'S NOT

you can be
nice and kind and sensitive
and still be a 'bad-ass'

you can care a little too much
and not be 'crazy'

you can double text and
tell them your feelings

you can be forward

or backwards
or sideways
or upside fucking down

you can wear rejection
like a crown that says
"hey at least i tried"

you don't have to fake it
till you make it
or keep 'showing up'
you can stay in bed
if you want

you can 'w e r k it'
or not, fix up or not
give a fuck or not

let's not let
pop culture teach us

that there is only one way to be
"100% that bitch."

SUMMER AND SKIN

why is it
that
as soon as
the sun arrives
for her favourite season

where skirts hang out
above the knees
and belly buttons
breathe easy

let out for air by crop tops
and sweaty skin
reveals itself for a yearly dose
of vitamin D

that we

become
walking targets

with velcro for catching words

like

'slut'

shot out of car windows

disguised as compliments
that nobody asked
for

as if our skin is not allowed
to enjoy the warmth
of a well awaited
summer

in all it's bare and beautiful
glory.

GREAT GRANNY'S EYES

from what i remember
they looked like DISCO BALLS
all silver and full of sass

and sometimes a little shattered too.

GLITTER

i like the way you say my name
you make it sound like
glitter
i don't know what glitter sounds like
apart from when you say my name.

HABITS

i've watched you
time and time again
fall
into the habit
of needing someone

of getting bored
of leaving
of being lonely
and of needing someone else

maybe you think
that this is love

but i think,
instead of breaking hearts

it would be easier
breaking bad habits.

THE GUY WHO FUCKED A BLACK GIRL

you came
and then you said

I JUST FUCKED A BLACK GIRL

as if the words warranted
a round of applause

you looked at me
as if i was about to pull
a trophy out from between my legs
or fire confetti from my nipples.

CHECK ON YOUR FRIENDS

ask me
if i'm ok
and i might lie
to you

but there's still more chance
that i'll tell the truth
than
if you don't ask me
at all.

TIP OF MY TONGUE

the rom-coms
promised me
i'd recognise it

instantly

this unexplained warmth
of familiarity
in our match

would set my entire
being ablaze
insulating the space
between my bones
with desire

this fire
raging

inextinguishable

there'd be this
pull
between us
like magnets

and the moment the penny
dropped would
feel like

someone paused the film

at its climax

my mouth would fill
with the taste of a
4 letter word
unmistakable

for anything other than

LOVE

that when i fell
for someone
for the first time
i wouldn't be able to help
but S C R E A M it
from the rooftops

and yet

it was nothing like that

in fact
it's taken 332 days
a maze of uncertainty
a phase of convincing myself
i was incapable

wondering
if it would ever happen

and then
last night
out of the blue
it did

unprompted

for the first time

i thought it

i felt it

and i was about to say it

when i realised

i like the way the words
fizz
like poppin' candy or sherbet
on the tip of my tongue

so i think i'll keep them there
instead.

PERSON

what if your person
never gets to be your person
because they're too busy
being some other person's
person

personally i think
that would be a shame.

PRETENDER

wow

for a second there
you really had me
believing in your

sweetness

it's funny isn't it
how much salt can
look like
sugar.

RUSH HOUR

while i was
minding my business
squeezed into the corner of a carriage
face pressed up against a window
inhaling breath
directly from strangers mouths

i realised that
yes,

we were forced together
far more intimately
than what we
may have chosen for ourselves

HOWEVER
THERE WAS NO NEED

for
your hands
that
found their place
on my lower back
slipped down into my lap
through the gap, between my legs

and your fingers
that
let's be honest

located themselves
FAR TOO CLOSE
to my labia

over the layers of clothes
i chose specifically
to keep
hands like those at bay

on a Monday morning
London rush hour.

SOFT

the soft folds
of my body
hold

my soul
my heart
my mind

wrap them
like gifts
inside

my skin
and bones

so yes,

they may stretch
and grow
change
shape and size
with age

crease and crumple
droop and drop

fold and fold again
as i grow old

but they will continue to
hold

my soul
my heart
my mind

and that, i find,

is a miracle.

I DON'T WANT

i don't want a
phone call or text or
a heartfelt letter
i don't need to hear that voice
feel those hands
lips
skin
i don't want your hoodie
(i'm not 15 anymore)

i don't want the photos
burn them if you like
set them on fire and watch
the smoke stir in the sky

delete the songs we danced to
there is no need
for a 'Happy Birthday'
to pop up on my Facebook timeline
once yearly

i don't even need my name
to spill from your lips
on nights when you've drunk
far too much gin

and i never
want to hear from our
'once mutual friends'
that
you still wear
the watch i gave you

pawn it
sell it
give it away

along with all your 'i'm sorries'

because the only thing i want is for
you to know

that
no matter how hard you tried
you did not break me,
and you will not break her
or her
or her.

APPLE JUICE

when i was a child
on sick days, at primary school
my grandmother used
to make hot apple juice,
sit on the end of the bed
and whisper 'it will get better'
until everything went warm

i'm not a child anymore,
but sometimes i still
make myself hot apple juice
whisper 'it will get better'
and wait

for everything to go warm.

THE PAST

in years to come
all of this
will just be memories

we
will look back
and laugh

longing
for the taste of our youth
to burn
on our tongues

the same way it did
when
the fire in our bellies

had only just begun to
spark.

PART 2

BRAVING WOMAN

LETTING GO

the only way i can describe it
is a thunderstorm
chaos
and endless rain
but the kind that was needed
after a long draught

to make everything
alive again.

SUNFLOWER STORY

when we first meet
they are everywhere

i wear them like
clips plaited
into the curl pattern
of my hair and you
pick bunches of them with pliers
that you sneak
through the gap in next door's
fence, while i invent a name for
every new shade of yellow
we discover

because somehow,
you see, what i see
which is that they are
all slightly different

then
at weekends
we walk amongst
fields of them,
floors and ceilings covered
parting only as our toes
trace pathways for
our feet
through bright yellow leaves

and
we keep the seeds
to bake bread, make oil
and press petals
into photo albums
filling scrapbooks
to nearly bursting

and i say aren't they
beautiful?
with my mouth full of homemade
sunflower margarine

and when i'm full
and my belly is a little
swollen
we speak about the future

about planting seeds in soil
for new growth
and i laugh
because i don't think we
will remember to water them

and i'm right
(like you always say i am)

we don't water them
so they never grow

and the following winter
you forget to bring them
inside so they freeze
over
and we only find one
shade of yellow
but neither of us remember
its name

not to mention
the lack of bread and oil
and my hair which
starts to coil in a different way
so that they
no longer fit into its style
after a while
all the albums are wrapped
like presents in a film of dust
left untouched and i struggle
to remember the last time
our fingers
pressed yellow flesh
softly into folds of recycled paper
let alone
each other's skin

and i begin to wonder
if they still exist
the sunflowers

if they were ever really
there in the first place
and we both cry, promise each other to
try and find them again

you bring me tulips
and i give you roses
and it's not that they're not
beautiful

they're just not the same

so we decide to leave it
to lovingly part ways
to move forwards,
move on

to let everything change
which it does

and a few years go by
till i see one again

a sunflower

but i still think of you.

DIFFERENCES

we used to stay home
playing Monopoly
and spend half the day
cooking up
elaborate meals to share
just between
the two of us

we'd eat

legs tucked up
and into each other
watching the Discovery Channel

but you,
you aren't like that

we drink red wine
smoke cigarettes
and listen to jazz

stay out all night
and have sex like strangers

and no matter how much i try
and convince myself
i know
that it just doesn't feel right

because when you touch me
all i can think about is
how much i wish
i could shed skin
like a snake

on the Discovery Channel.

DESPITE HERSELF

although

she would always be the first
to call out
patriarchal bullshit
it did still catch her eye

on the corner shop shelf

the headline
in crispy pink lettering

stuck to the front of a
five side spread
glossy paper magazine
that read

"WHAT DO MEN LOOK FOR IN WOMEN?"

and despite herself

that night she went home
and strip searched her body
for the answers.

SHIT COFFEE

you say
why don't they just
realise that they're wrong?

and i say
you wouldn't want to
'wake up and smell the coffee'
if the one you drink
tastes of hate
if it's frothed with fascism
sweetened with white supremacy
and finished off with a hint
of homophobia
honey,
everyone knows prejudice stinks.

SILENCE

silence
is a choice
i made

knowing that if i
spoke

the words
of the moment
would be dripping
in hatred

and there is already enough of that
in the world.

MADE IT

"you made it"
she squeezed my hand
and whispered

the past two years
swirled around the inside
of my stomach
like a whirlpool

its water
rose up
and spilled over the edges of my eyes
raced down my cheeks
and got caught in my smile

i gripped onto the sides of the chair
waiting
for the floor to drop from beneath me

"breathe"
she said

i exhaled
and let my lungs
fill
with the beginnings
of a new chapter

and with that breath
i finally made it.

WHY

why do we teach
children so much
about the importance
of 'bravery'

of the brave prince
who saves the princess
from the tower
guarded by
the fire breathing dragon
and never cries
when he falls over

like fear and pain
are the enemy

and we should
all be running head first
into burning buildings?

OUR VERSION

i think
that in our version
of the story,
we somehow

skipped the start
or just thought
'fuck it'
and tore
the whole book apart

flipped the lid on
Pandora's box
just to
enjoy the chaos of
seeing everything

spilt

like ink
taken straight from the
pages
of the middle chapter

where the drama is

where the secrets run free

like the skeletons

we
unlocked in
each other's cupboards

when we carved open our
hearts

after promising ourselves
we wouldn't

knowing that
sharing their contents
would tip the scales
from strangers

into something

neither of us
were
looking for

we didn't follow
the narrative

ignored the timeline

went a little
more L to Y
than A to B

knowing that the only certainty
was the ending

waiting just around the corner

so yeah,

i haven't read many
stories like this one

and i think that makes sense

cos

i haven't met many people
like you.

AFTER WORK WINE

i think sometimes
(not always)

the wisest of words
come doused
in white wine
from the mouths of
women
who have had
a hard day at work.

HAZELNUT

it turns out
that

at the end of the day,
year or even decade

there is still
no way
for me

to wish you

into wanting

to know about

my favourite ice cream
flavour or why i hate
animated films
and find it weirdly
satisfactory to sip tea
from the
tip of a teaspoon

or talk in rhyme
and write poems
and find
T-shirts
with random slogans

stuck to the front of
them so fun to wear

why i never sit still
for too long,
or bite my lip till it's nearly
bleeding
just to concentrate

why i sometimes take
every little
word to heart
and let it indent
like scars on its already
bruised surface

and ask for forgiveness
for things i never did wrong

i can't pray,
you paying those things
attention, into existence

no matter how hard
i hope
it won't be enough
to change

what is an already

made up
moved on
mind

but i know
that there are millions
(ok maybe not millions)
but still
so many people
in the world

who would want
to know

that it's

hazelnut

my favourite ice cream
flavour

they might even want to
share a tub with me
while we
watch a
(non animated) film
and when i say sorry
for
something as

insignificant

as eating the last spoonful

they'll know
that i'm still working on it
without me having
to wish it true.

MOON AND SUN

every summer

at 4:39am
the early morning
moon
shines through
my crisp cut curtains
on its way down to
trade places
with the sun
so she can
'do her thing' in the day time

they pass each other
for the briefest moment

just long enough

for the moon
to kiss her good morning
as she whispers
a joyous good night

they have risen and set
like this for years

at first
i thought it was tragic
that they would never get to live

together in the sky

but now i realise

they would not be happy
if they did

for

sometimes powerful things

need a solitary place
to exist.

WRINKLES

the wrinkles
on your face
are imprints on your skin

of all the times you have felt something
strongly enough
to turn the corners of your mouth
into a smile

to drop your jaw in disbelief
or raise your eyebrows in utter excitement

the times every facial muscle
contracted in pain or grief
and your eyes squinted to notice every
detail of your loved one's body

these are the marks
you have collected from the moments and
milestones in your life

written on your face

do not be tricked into tippex-ing over them
in white cream

from a jar labelled "anti-ageing."

BEAUTIFUL BOUQUET OF WOMEN

and when it gets messy and mixed up like paint scattered across
a canvas
women like you have taught me
that we are all just making abstract art
the kind that will turn out to be worth a fortune in the end
fierce and forward moving
all fists and two fingers in the face of resistance
your words like waves, full of salt and grit
spill from lips that speak in sharp tongues
and far too many swear words
you have souls built for shattering glass ceilings
hands made to carry the future
your stories they are skyscrapers
tall buildings
made of bricks and bravery,
as you continue to grow and blossom
like flowers
i thank the universe, that i found a bunch like you,
a beautiful bouquet of women.

SISTER

she looked at me
and forced a smile

a wobbly, quivering smile
but a smile none the less
followed by a deep breath
and the words "i'm fine"

so

i took her hand
and reminded her
that it's okay
because
there are things even lions
are scared of.

TO THE NUTRITIONIST I WAS ONCE
SHIT SCARED OF

i don't know if you
realise that you saved me
made me believe
that there was something
worth fighting
for,
you saw a person beyond
the scared and slightly
sassy girl
that broke the rules

you made me laugh, let me cry
gave me the space that i needed
to fight and it always felt
like you stood somewhere
in my corner,
cheering me on
but also ready to call me out
when i was wrong

(i needed that)

you sat with me, in a Costa
and didn't question the tears that
splashed into my coffee
instead we
talked about nails and clothes

(side note; you always wore the coolest)

you weren't easy on me
you saw what i could be
if i learnt to channel the energy
into the right things

and we laughed
a lot

which i find kind of crazy -
given the severity of the situation

i wish i was better at thank yous
because not to sound dramatic
i couldn't have done it without you

and i know it's your job
and i didn't always make it easy
but you taught me
that some people truly just want to help

and that felt..... scary (nice)

sometimes i still get the urge to
call you when i've managed an
unplanned piece of chocolate cake
at 4:00am after a night out

(don't worry i know that's inappropriate)

and i don't even have your number

but sometimes i have this voice
in my head, that says

'come on, you can do it'

and it sounds a lot like yours.

SEARCHING

i am seeking, searching
for a story,

one a little
like my own

a face
fixed with fury
and frustration
eyes
with the same scale
lenses
and ears that have heard the
word

"different"

ring through their drums

like an orchestra
playing
its crescendo

i am seeking, searching
for a knowing smile

a shared tear, fear
laughter

a hand, whose hold
says i've been there

more than any words ever could.

BRIDGES

of course
there will be darkness
when you have
wasted so much
of the fire
within you,

on burning bridges

DREAM

the way we spent
our Saturday evening
pretending

left me

far too tired
to walk away

so yet again
i chose to stay

to shut my eyes
tight enough to hide
the sign
that flashed
'REALITY'
in all its neon glory

rolled over to my side
of the bed, and
buried my head in a pillow of
'you'll get through it'

drew a breath to
whisper a 'goodnight'
that should have been
a 'goodbye'

traded
falling in love
for falling asleep
and had
another dream

knowing it was you,
i needed to wake up from.

SAYING IT

mother,

i watched
you

slowly
softly
but so certainly

unravel the truth

pull back the curtain

on what
they had buried
in years of denial
and defence

and now

i must write
all the words

that even
i was afraid of reading

for if i don't

who will?

STAND STILL

stand still

silence, windows open to
the sounds of sirens,
running taps, chapped hands
heroes in numbers, numbness
and news which we switch
on and off,
and on, and off

offering

words of comfort
in texts, filled with emojis,
posters and small hands
waving from windows
waiting, wishing
for time to tend to crisis,
and spin the earth
quickly towards 'this is over'

countless flaws
in connection as another
screen is frozen, and another
signal spun like thin gold,
starts to fizz and flicker
as the picture disappears
along
with the evenings

that dissolve into
sleepless nights as we toss
and turn and our stomachs churn
with worry for the the future
and yet

it is still spring

somehow
the sun still shines
in her shyness, half warmth
whispering in the ears
of summer
as she dances the tango
with a gentle breeze -
dodging the birds
who also still sing -

so stand still
for a second
and see
that somehow

it's still spring.

COVID FEAR

it's scary
seeing
how quickly our grips loosen
on compassion and community
almost as though
it slips off our skin
along with all
the soap and water

like kindness
evaporates in the
2 to 3 metre space we must
keep between us

and that mouths covered with
masks can no longer speak
mercifully

surely we must still hold each other
not with our hands

but with our hearts.

SIBLINGS

you steal my clothes
you steal my food
but *always* you steal my heart.

COUNT YOURSELF

when you achieve
what it is

that you
set out to achieve

don't

'count yourself lucky'

instead

'count yourself fucking
magnificent'

MONSTERS

when you are little
you think that the scariest monsters
are the ones with horns
and claws
and 3,000 eyes
that you read about in story books

but then

when you get older
you realise
that the scariest monsters
were actually the ones
that looked
just like the people

who were your protectors.

HOW

how can you steal
from us,
beat us, kill us
tie our hands
behind our backs
until we surrender,
for simply existing
say
we are the problem
but our music is not, our fashion
is not, our hairstyles our not
how can you strip us of everything
we've got -

and walk away

wearing our culture on your backs
and our blood on your hands
our last breaths
between your fingers -

fists,

that force our
faces into the ground
how can you stand the sound
of unjust bullets, piercing through
gentle hearts
or even just stand on the

sideline -

silent

saying nothing
or cross the road
or lock us up or knock us down
or drive us out of another town
or stop and search or sexualise
or claim to be scared for your
own lives

like we're the thugs
and we're the threat

because the boy waving
the banner above his head

is really the brute

and the mother who says
'please don't shoot'

is the monster

and the many who march
for the many they lost
are those who use murder at any cost

don't tell us you're scared
with a gun in your hand
and the means to use
violence

to keep your "promised land".

WOMANHOOD

but this

womanhood

is
not just

the curves,
the breasts
or the bleeding
between my legs

the stomach ready to stretch
and baby bearing hips
luscious lips

hair
eyes
skin, flesh

it cannot
be measured in
cup sizes
in 'tightness'
or sex appeal

because

this
womanhood

is somewhere
so deep
within me

that even you can't see it.

ASKING FOR HELP

somehow the words were always there
lost,
adrift, sinking
in the quick sand of
suppression
of push it down
and bottle it up
and sell it
with a receipt for the rest
of the world
signed
'i'm fine'

the words were always there
trapped in the bubbles
in the pockets
too afraid to be empty
of the tiniest
pieces of change
you'd have traded
if you felt
that someone
somewhere
spoke your language

and now
the words are still here
still swirling
in the air of the world

you no longer dance in

and i pray the next time
these words find their way
on to the tip
of another's tongue
this world gives them
the space and support
to say them.

TRUST

if you can't
trust me
when i say
it gets easier

then please

just try and
trust me
when i say
i have been there

and then look

at how i am still standing.

LOOK UP

when it seems
like the odds

are stacked against you

look up

count the clouds

if every one of those
has a silver lining

you,
must be sitting on a fortune.

MAYBE ONE DAY

i always wonder
if it's a 'maybe one day' kind of thing, a maybe someday,
sort of affair, that there
is a chance that the future's bright
that we might, maybe -
make something stick
that it's a bit "they'll end up together"
"it's written in the stars"
and though it makes me sick to say it
i hope the term 'soulmates' gets thrown around,
when they talk about us
i hope someone says 'i better be invited to the wedding'
not knowing that we're too anti-establishment
to ever say i do, but i do
think about it, marked in the diary for years down the line
when you see me in a coffee shop
and say that you never forgot that i only take decaf
and that's followed by some mumbles about how neither of us
have changed, and before we know it we've engaged
in 20 minutes of conversation and the guy in the queue behind
will be getting inpatient and we'll go to grab the sugar at the
same time and your hand will caress mine
and both of us might actually have time,
to stay a while and a while will turn into forever, slowly
the way grapes turn into wine
and we'll be like that bottle
that sat on the shelf for years,
fermenting, cementing,
something so concrete

cos it's taken years to build,
and you didn't have the tools to tell me the truth
and i got trigger happy with my feelings
drilling i love you's in to your yet too scared to hear ears
and you did the classic -
shut down, abandon, shake your head till the memory of me
dissolves, become so involved in your self and your life
and your living
and like anyone would, i kinda hate you for a while,
i'm jealous of the way you get away unscathed and i hate
myself for longing for someone who categorically says he
doesn't want me,
and it goes on for a while till i finally walk away
and as i'm turning the corner onto the road of move on,
my phone pings, and your name titles a text
'i'm in town, do you wanna grab coffee?'
and we do
of course we do
we always do
and you remember all the details
you somehow know the script
verbatim of a story i told you 3 years ago
and it's almost like you haven't forgotten
like you've been finding yourself thinking about me too
and i want to make a move but i don't
cos there's only so many times i can take being told
that i'm just a mate
while you simultaneously state
all the reasons why you were so happy when you met me,

you reminisce and laugh
and get a bit awkward and we drink the final sips
and you say "i'll see you soon"
and for us soon means a year or so
and it'll go on like that
and at some point i'll meet someone and almost actually get
used to the idea
and then i'll hear on the grapevine that you've met someone too
and i won't get out of bed for a few days
i'll make a list of all the reasons why this is for the best,
make peace i guess
wish you well with a slightly bitter taste in my mouth
and more months will pass like pedestrians do a coffee shop
window
the same one where we meet again
and your hand caresses mine and both of us might actually
have time,
to stay a while and a while will turn into forever, slowly
the way grapes turn into wine and this time,
you're ready and i'm a bit scared
but you grab my hand and say something cringe like
"we'll make it work"
and by some bloody miracle we will
see, i wonder if this is all just ageing,
that fate functions best on a good few years of back and forth
of fucking up, of forgetting, of accepting, of collecting
pieces of a story,
we'll tell at a dinner party one day
when someone asks how we got together.

WHY IT IS NOT A RACE

this is a reminder
that
this life is not a race

it is not a sprint towards
some sort of finish line

you do not have to stay
stuck
in your own lane

doing laps of the same track

sometimes

there will only be
a few people
cheering from the side lines

you will get tired
and over taken and defeated

you may trip
or have a thousand false starts

you will probably get lost
and tired of seeing the people ahead of
you

but that's ok

stop

take your time

go the scenic route
and enjoy the view

because the truth is

you will never run faster
than your own legs can carry you anyway.

NOT ALL GREAT ART

not all
great art
has to be born
out of suffering
and
not all great stories
need to be rooted
in pain
just like,
not every calm
must follow a storm
and not every heart
is supposed to be
broken

maybe, we
sometimes
have a habit of forgetting
that there is just as much to learn
from joy
as there is from grief.

HAPPY ENDINGS

we are raised on
fairytales and disney films

this means
we are raised on

happy endings and grand finales

but i think

the rest of the story is just as important.

With a special thanks to Susanna and Saphira Wing for the cover art, Graham Scott at Human Design for the cover composition, Tom Barrett at TBA and Shane Rhodes at Wrecking Ball Press. Lastly to my family, both biological and chosen, thank you for your unwavering belief in my work.

Talitha Wing possesses a powerful voice and the honest, raw and intimate nature of the poetry in this debut collection will make a positive impact on your life.

Within the pages of *The Things I Learnt and the Things I Still I Don't Know About*, Talitha presents a collection of work that provides a voice for those who, like her, refuse to be categorised and labelled. Talitha explores the ambiguities of the journey into adulthood, self-acceptance and what it means to be 'other' in a manner that will resonate with readers.

Poets can spend years finding their voice but Talitha writes with the same level of self-assurance, passion and determination that are evident in her spoken word performances. We should all be thankful that she's picked up her weapon of choice in order to get these poems onto the page and is now ready to share them with the world. *The Things I Learnt and the Things I Still I Don't Know About* is as vital and exhilarating as poetry gets.

"Messy, sticky, and bloody beautiful!" - Dean Atta

ISBN 978-1-9031108-3-6

9 781903 110836

£10.00